# Revealed:
# 6 Kumite (Sparring) Tactics That Make A Champion

By

**Sensei Efezino Akpotu**

4th Degree Black Belt

# Table of Contents

About the author

Copyright

Chapter 1
    Introduction

Chapter 2
    You can be the best and perform at your best always

CHAPTER 3
    Tactic number 1: Before attacking your opponent, sufficiently break their concentration.

CHAPTER 4
    Tactic Number 2: When your opponent is attacking, bridging and intercepting them swiftly is your scoring chance!

CHAPTER 5
    Tactic 3: Attack with high speed combination aggressively

CHAPTER 6
    Tactic 4: Develop and use your footwork to prevent your opponent's best techniques and tactics.

CHAPTER 7
    TacticNumber 5: Make your body memorize your attacking patterns.

CHAPTER 8
    Tactic Number 6: Never pass up opportunities to take advantage of your opponent's mistakes

# About The Author

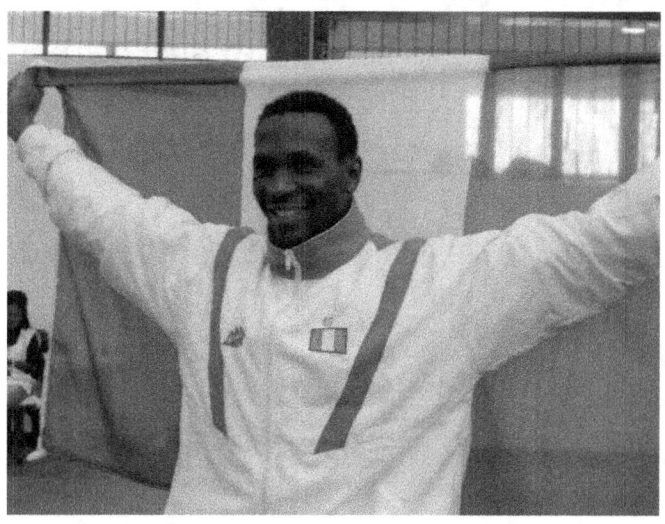

**Sensei Efezino Akpotu**

(4th Degree Black Belt)

Efezino Akpotu is a retired Nigerian Elite International Athlete.

He represented Nigeria at many All Africa Games and several other international and world championships in Karate, Taekwondo and Kickboxing.

A world Silver Medalist at the WKA World Championships in Karlsruhe, Germany (2007) and many times African and National champion.

**Copyright © 2021 by Efezino Akpotu**

All rights reserved. No part of this publication may be reproduced, distributed, or transmitted in any form or by any means, including photocopying, recording, or other electronic or mechanical methods, without the prior written permission of the publisher, except in the case of brief quotations embodied in critical reviews and certain other noncommercial uses permitted by copyright law.

For permission requests, write to the owner.

**Contact below:**

Email: senseiefezino@gmail.com
WhatsApp: +234 8080 224 596

# Chapter 1

## Introduction

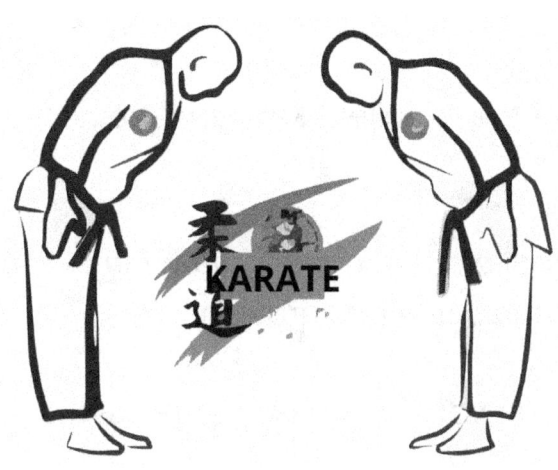

They say success leaves clues and this is so true.

There is a pattern to success in karate just as it is in every other worthwhile endeavor in the world. Thankfully, I lived it and got some great results.

And the pattern is predictable because it worked for me and my siblings, and it keeps working for my students that I train.

Therefore, the following pattern will certainly deliver similar results to you as well.

My name is Efezino Akpotu, I started karate fairly late in my teens, 17 years of age to be exact. My older brother was 19 at the time. And our younger brother was 11.

Our dad indirectly fueled our passion and gave us pictures of what we eventually wanted to be like, though unknowingly to him...

He would usually buy lots of Martial Arts movies for us. The likes of Jean Claude Van Damme, Jackie Chan, Bruce Lee, Donnie Yen, Yen Bao, Sammo Hung, Cynthia Ruthrock, Michelle Yeoh etc..
And we loved them to the moon.. we would watch all day and start kicking flowers all over our compound until the landlord threatened us with quit notice.

Dad played a great influence in our lives.. But what he didn't know was how to connect us to a coach to harness our passion constructively.

However, somehow, we crossed paths with karate instructors who eventually built us up.

Shihan Emmanuel Onuegbu was one of the excellent karate instructors that trained us.

And we continued until we got connected to a bigger club run by the Rivers state (Nigeria) coach at the time, Shihan Izonebi Masarawon.

There as junior ranks we would usually be very competitive against the seniors in sparring and all.
Then we would attend all the state tournaments.

I recall one bitter but the best experience I had at the first state championships I attended in 1996.

My Dad came to watch us. Just before my bout my dad stepped out to quickly get something. Before he returned I was done competing...
I had lost against a very aggressive opponent..

He beat me 6:0 and it was so quick that the bout ended in less than 1 or 2 minutes..

This was devastating to my young mind.
A lot of things went through my mind.
"How could I lose just like that", that was my thought.

My dad returned and was surprised I was done. He asked how was it? I said I lost!
He pat me on the back and assured "you will do better next time"

He himself was an athlete and a sports teacher who ran in Sprints athletics for his state (Old Bendel State) when the National Stadium of Nigeria in Lagos was opened in 1973.
He was also a very passionate Lawn Tennis Player who won some great trophies playing leisurely in Port Harcourt.

So, the tournament ended for me in just a few moments.

I went home empty handed in my weight category..
I can't really recall what the results were in the team events.

Luckily, someone sowed a seed and PRINCIPLE of greatness in my mind.

He came around and talked to me a bit. And he said these words to me: "If you train more and harder you will always do better".

This sounded so important to me. This was the remedy my young mind longed for to calm my total disappointment after that loss.
I took that word and knitted it in my soul and spirit.
And my body received the aftermath transformation.

The words: "If you train more and harder you will always do better".
That became my watch word.


Leaving that tournament, I went home to a regime of consistent training.

I would usually keep practicing what the coach had taught many nights I would be practicing. Even in our bedroom.

My brothers would join.
Soon our friends would join us in the evening to practice.

That was consistency!

And don't forget, we already had a vision and a picture of being a champion from the many Martial Arts movies we were watching. we loved seeing Van Damme become a champion in the Movie, Blood Sport; Lauren Avadon become champion in, King of the Kickboxer etc

Unsurprisingly, most of our friends who started training with us, even though they usually followed us to the karate club, they didn't have the strong mental picture we had.
So almost all of them quit karate.

From the next championships I and my siblings consistently became state champions with superior performances.

And eventually all three of us became national champions, and eventually two of us became international champions until my younger sibling started pursuing a career in Medicine ( He is currently a Sports doctor though and a prominent Sports council management official in our adopted state, Bayelsa, In Nigeria..
Of course, I went on to become many times national and international champion for my country Nigeria in karate, Taekwondo, kickboxing and Kungfu.

Being a multiple sports national champion In a country like Nigeria is significant. Why so? Because we have a massive population (over 120 Million) and a great deal of karate and Martial Arts practitioners..

Emerging as a champion in such a country tells of consistency on the part of the champion..

One very important aspect of my journey was the fact that, even though I was young, I somehow had the Wisdom to look for athletes and coaches who had great results in the Martial Arts.. I was paying some of them to teach me.
I was fortunate to train with great guys like:

1. Wayne Otto O.B.E. (9 time British world karate Champion)

2. Frank Brennan (British world karate Champion)

3. Julian Tourney (British world Karate Champion.

4. Andy Sherry (Trainer of karate champions).

5. Kenosuke Enoeda (Trainer of karate Champions)

6. Joel (7 times Cuban Pan-America Karate Champion

7. Roland Conar (German World Kickboxing Champion)

8. Alfred Ohimain (Trainer of champions)

9. Shihan Izonebi Masarawon
10. Shihan Segun Abode (Karate Champion)
11. Shihan Jegede Dave (Karate tactician)
12. Shihan Emmanuel Onuegbu
13. Sanbon Mene Mubana (Taekwondo Champion)
14. Sabon Frank Foubiri (Taekwondo Champion)
15. Sabon Kuro Okorowanta (Taekwondo Champion)
16. Kalamu (kickboxing Coach)
17. Seiji Nishimura (Japanese world karate champion and trainer of champions)
18. Shihan Segun Akinola (Coach and Champion)
19. Shihan Vitalis Dirioyema
20. Sensei Kingsley Duke Onuelu (Champion)
21. Sensei Lugard Osayi (Champion)
22. Sensei John Ogwo (Champion)
23. Sabon Osmos Isaac (Taekwondo)
24. Sabon Ibrahim Yahuza (Taekwondo)
25. Master Ferguson Oluigbo (Taekwondo)
26. Blessing Ichioma Akpotu (Champion)

These men and more imparted so much knowledge, wisdom and tactics to improve my game.
I'm forever grateful for their impact and influence.

I would be right and correct to say I out-trained everyone in Nigeria during my time. The results showed.

I would usually finish an entire karate tournament without conceding a single point.
It even extended to one international competition in Lomê Togo in 2005 when I was almost at the prime of my game.
This is like winning 3 gold medals without conceding a single point.
It drove the crowd and the media crazy that they were looking for me all over until they tracked me where we lodged..

I also recall solely representing Nigeria at the African Karate Championships in Durban South Africa in 2004 after emerging from a training camp of over 34 invited athletes of Nigeria's finest Athletes.

Shamefully, lack of funds made it happen that we only needed to be represented by just one athlete..

Consistency took me to a lot of international championships like the French Open karate Championships, The French Open Taekwondo Championship, the WKA World Championships in Karlsruhe, Germany, The World Taekwondo Championships in Copenhagen, Denmark, The WAKO World Kickboxing Champion in Skopjè, Macedonia, I also represented, Nigeria at 3 All Africa Games in Abuja, Algiers (Algeria) and Maputo (Mozambique) and others.

Only consistency would have done these.
And it should suffice to say, a strong Vision also played a role..

If you saw a pattern already, then that's it.

**Here again are some of the benefits you will be getting:**

1. How to Never pass up opportunities to take advantage of your opponent's errors!

2. How to smartly shorten the journey for you to become a consistent champion and the best.

3. How to out train your peers with undying motivation and be in the top 1% of high performers in the world

4. How to take full advantage of footwork that puts the most formidable opponents specialties to nought.

5. Understand the dynamics of perfect timing for fail proof counter techniques by coming within range when your opponent attacks.

6. How to pressure your opponent to attack you while his defenses are vulnerable to your super counter abilities.

7. Confidence in posture as a great athlete.

8. Achieve a state of expertise and confidence where you can perform your best at all times.

9. Gain the rare ability to judge your opponents without making mistakes.

10. You will learn to make your body memorize the basic attacking pattern you will need to become a champion.

11. You will know exactly when to make attacks that have high chances of success.

12. You will know exactly when to counter your opponents no matter their level of expertise.

13. You will learn how to force your opponent to make errors and take them as your chances.

But I will take time to explain every single step on the way to your Success.

# Chapter 2

## You can be the best and perform at your best always

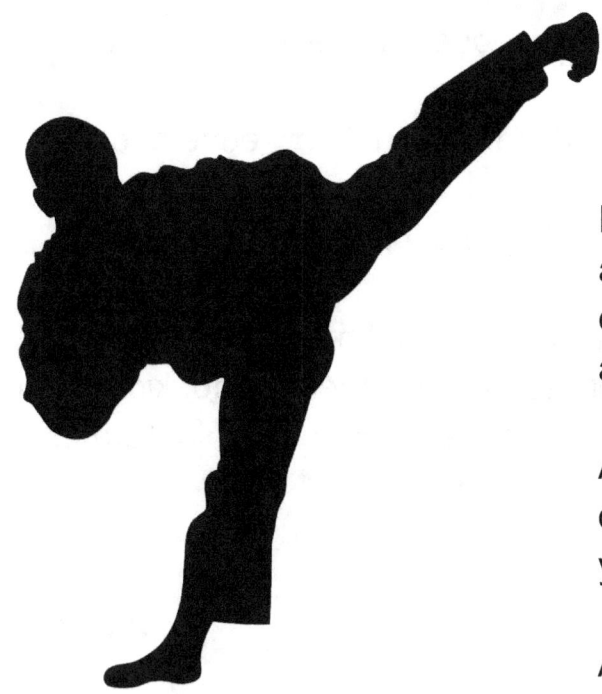

Do you have great karate dreams and expectations for yourself and don't know exactly how to go about attaining the required skill level?

Are you worried that your huge dreams may not turn out the way you desire them to be in karate?

Are you worried your skill level hasn't won you a karate tournament medal or first place yet?

Did any Karate coach or anyone put you down on the basis of your skill level?

It's ok if you experience all these negative things, but here is what is wrong: not knowing exactly what to do about it to turn the odds in your favor.

I am bold to assure you that my experiences and skill level can help you reach your goals.
Why?

Because. I have helped many athletes become national and international champions from Nigeria.

*These 6 sparring tactics is the game changer for everyone I have trained.*

No matter your past or experience level, you will succeed with these proven tactics.

My biggest desire and fulfillment is to see those with desire and hunger become their best.
And it is insanely possible with the right information, knowledge and guidance.
And that's exactly what you are likely going to get if you do things right.

The top 6 tactics most people don't know about that made me a national champion across 4 martial arts disciplines: Karate, Taekwondo, kickboxing & Kungfu; and also made me represent Nigeria at world level in Karate, Taekwondo and Kickboxing.

**These are some of the great benefits you will gain from this material:**

1. You will know exactly when to make attacks that have high chances of success rate
2. You will know exactly when to counter your opponents no matter their level of expertise
3. How to Never pass up opportunities to take advantage of your opponent's errors!
4. How to smartly shorten the journey for you to become a consistent champion and the best.
5. How to out train your peers with undying motivation and be in the top 1% of high performers in the world
6. How to take full advantage of footwork that puts the most formidable opponents specialties to nought.
7. Understand the dynamics of perfect timing for fail proof counter techniques by coming within range when your opponent attacks.
8. How to pressure your opponent to make mistakes; to attack you while his defenses are vulnerable to your super counter abilities.
9. Achieve a state of expertise and confidence
where you can perform your best at all times..
10. Gain the rare ability to judge your opponents without making mistakes.
11. You will learn to make your body memorize the basic attacking pattern you will need to become a champion!
12. You will know exactly when to make attacks that have high chances of success rate
13. You will know exactly when to counter your opponents no matter their level of expertise.
14. Learn how to force your opponent to make errors and take them as your chance.
15. Confidence in posture as a great athlete.

# CHAPTER 3

**Tactic 1**: Before attacking your opponent, sufficiently break their concentration.

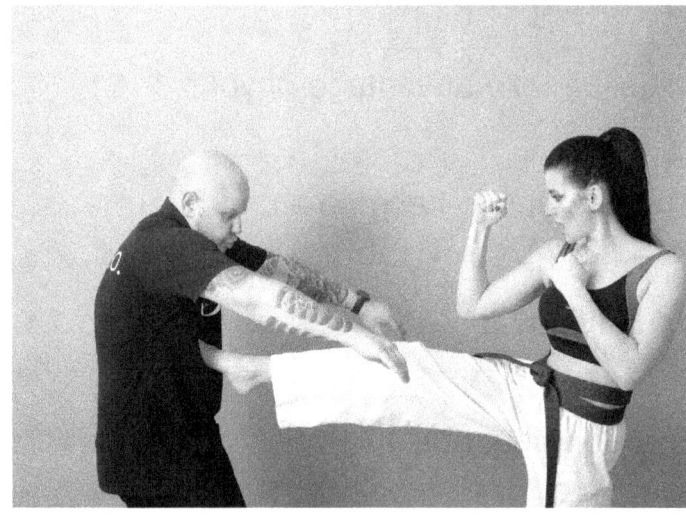

You don't want to move into your opponent's space with their awareness and concentration fully in place.

Entering their space without breaking their concentration will always trigger their counter or reaction technique to your disadvantage. That can't guarantee you reaching your target on their body.

Infact, you will get scored by a good reaction or counter fighter.

The only thing that gives you a chance to score on a good opponent is to break their concentration.

How do you do that?

**Some of my concentration breaking patterns are:**

1. When bouncing in front of your opponent with all the feints and pulling activities going on, cunningly, as if you are relaxed and not ready for an attack, make a footwork deviation of about 30 to 45 degrees from the straight line that connects both of you frontally. They will be forced to turn or adjust to face you.

At that split second of them turning to face you is your chance of raining some fast combination of techniques on them. Ensure to vary the levels( chudan and Jordan).

This momentary movement breaks their concentration and allows you to attack into their space and target. You must practice very well with understanding and swiftness.

2. Bouncing in front of your opponent, do a wave like motion by leaning your head and upper body and returning like a wave form and then spring forward with your combination of techniques as you complete the waveform motion.

That motion is so deceptive that it will almost call out the opponent but make them relax back as they monetarily see you leaving the circle.

At the point of that relaxation is when you are attacking them. That breaks the concentration of your opponent a great deal once you fully understand and master the pattern.

3. While bouncing In front of your opponents, intentionally transform to a "to and fro" bouncing movement , and do it cunningly as if you are not up to anything. But with the intention of turning one of the "to and fro" movement as a bridge close to your opponent and attack from the front of the movement not from the back of the movement.  Many opponents don't see it and it's difficult for them to counter.

4. You can momentarily tap or cease the lead gloves of your opponent and let go. While their reaction is to recover the hand, you are attacking at the moment they are recovering their hand from the tap or hold of their hand. That's another breaking of the concentration pattern.

5. Another pattern is conditioning their minds towards expecting a front leg sweep or tap from your own front leg, but your intention is to attack Jordan Kizami tsuki and chudan gyaku tsuki.

Ofcourse, you can come up with other patterns following the principle above. Deception and show one thing and do another. If you understand, train and Master these patterns, you will always easily make attacks that will make clean scores.

# CHAPTER 4

## Tactic 2: When your opponent is attacking, bridging and intercepting them swiftly is your striking chance

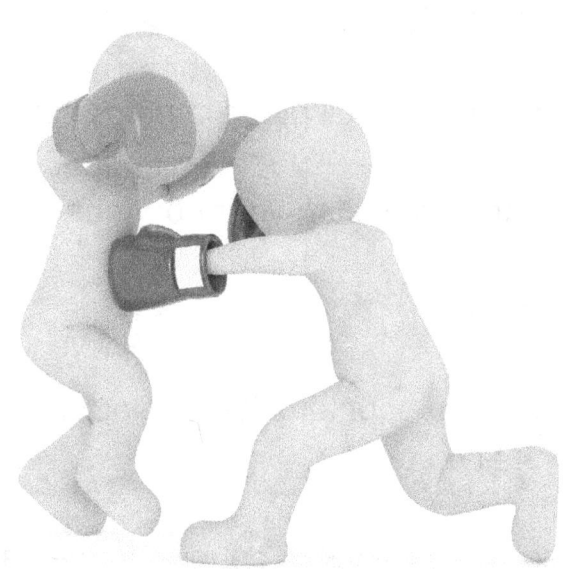

It is unavoidable not to have your protection or defense weaken when attacking. Therefore, train your body and mind to take advantage for instantaneous counters at the moment your opponent moves in attack.

However, you will have the best chance to intercept if you are the one that forced or provoked them to attack by pulling or squeezing or feinting them.

**Some of the techniques to train as counter are:**

1. kizami tsuki. (Lead hand jab)
2. Gyaku tsuki (reverse punch)
3. Uraken Uchi (back fist strike)
4. Jordan Kizami Mawashi geri (lead leg roundhouse kick face level)
5. Ushiro geri (turn back kick)
6. etc

You have to practice these with a partner until you master the principle of interception or coming within range. And it must have a good distance to make a valid karate score.

You want to counter just about when the opponent is taking off so that your timing and distancing are right and correct for a valid score.

Note: You will need speed training using elastic bands, reflex training and lean muscle training using light weights to enhance your chances of swift interception of your opponents.

Always stay one step ahead of
your opponent. Know your distance and timing.

Never wait for your opponent to attack with their full plans in place. You must
move forward in pulls or feints, forcing and provoking your opponent to attack or you'll
never have the best opportunity to counter.

Again, note that you could do an interception counter without blocking their technique. And you can also do a block and counter.

Don't block to retreat and then counter; rather block to counter immediately or your timing won't be right!

# CHAPTER 5

**Tactic 3: Attack with high speed combination aggressively**

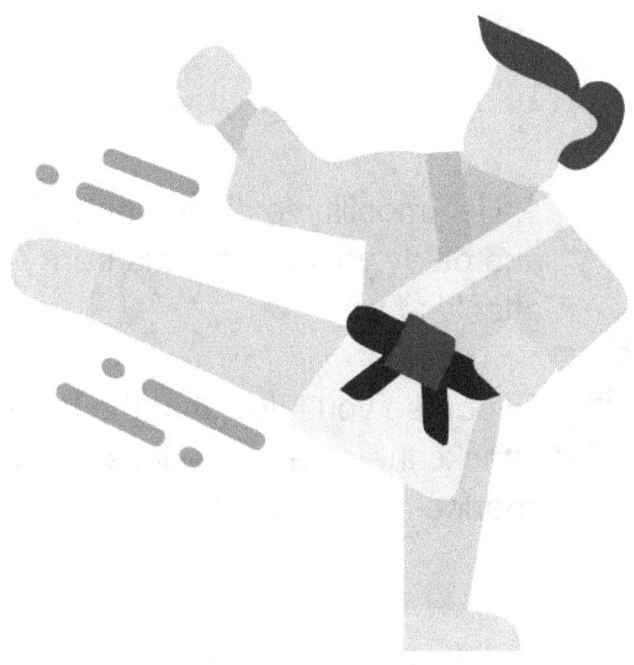

The combination of techniques you want to use during fighting must be developed by practicing them consistently. Practice slowly for good form. Once your body memorizes the combination pattern which happens over time, you start building tremendous speed for that combination of techniques.

For instance: I have a favorite combination of Kizami, gyaku tsuki, and ura-mawashi geri.

I recall taking time to practice it with little speed, moderate speed and super speed. Of course, have the consciousness of correctness of form.
So before attacking with such a combination, you want to sufficiently break the opponent's concentration to allow entrance into his space with a fast and furious speed of light combination.

You could have all 3 of your combinations of techniques make targets and score. It used to be a common place for me when I was competing.

The secret is, thoroughly break your opponents concentration momentarily before attacking.

# CHAPTER 6

**Tactic 4: Develop and use your footwork to prevent your opponent's best techniques and tactics.**

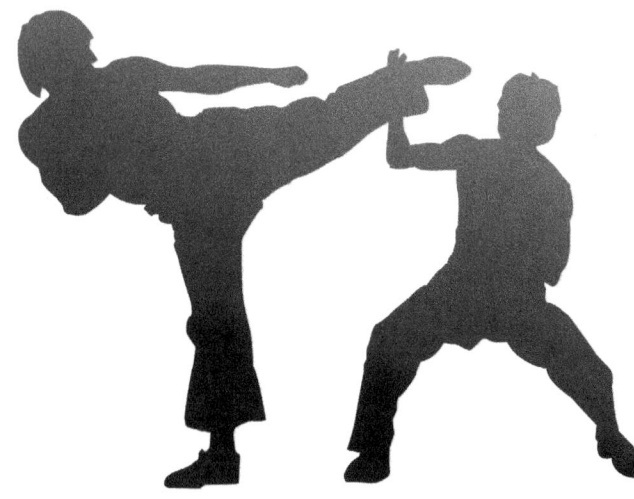

**Two things are involved:**

1. Use mobility to disorganized and delay your opponents from attacking you.

Of course you know that the less attacks they make, the lesser their chances of making a score on you.

So you want to develop footwork that supports your constant mobility so that you are a moving target.

You need to be a very difficult fighter for your opponents. Developing great footwork for constant mobility will be a game changer for you.

2. Use footwork for angular evasions and counter attacks.

Your ability to make angular evasions cannot be over-emphasized, especially when your opponent is attacking.

And you should be able to do a counter attack after evasion. You could use single techniques like Kizami tsuki, gyaku tsuki, uraken Uchi or even a combination of pinches and kicks.

**Some of the evasion patterns are:**

1. You could move sideways. And swiftly, left or right.

2. You could take a step backwards before angling out.

3. You could slide backwards before angling out.

4. Depending on the thrusts of the opponent towards you, you could step back, and then slide before angling out.

Don't forget, a counter is always your chance. Don't always angle in in same direction all the time so as to prevent being read by your opponent and their coach

So, remember that you don't have to allow your opponents to attack you with their full preparation and plan in place.

You want them to attack prematurely by forcing them to do so. You pull them with feints by entering into their territory.

So they will be forced to throw some techniques out at you. Whereas you have a plan to angle out and counter, especially if they are fast and have furious combinations.

You don't want to fight such people in a straight line.

You have to consistently practice and develop these patterns and it will stick to you.

Foot work requires some strong leg muscles. You will need to build those calf muscles, quadriceps (thigh muscles) hamstrings and other leg muscles by using weights and climbing stairs. I did all that consistently.

**You also need some agility training**

1. Skipping for up to 30 minutes or 1 hour.
2. jump ropes (i usually tie a rope my knee level between two points and jump over to and fro without double bouncing. I just jump continuously over it. I would usually do reps of 100 and above for 3 to 5 sets.

For a more difficult jump rope I would tie it as high as my waist level to jump. Do as much as you can and increase reps and sets as you get better at it. I would also do
3. Jumping jacks 100 reps and more for 3 to 5 sets with speed.

You should do other agility training as well.

# CHAPTER 7

**Tactic 5: Make your body memorize your attacking patterns.**

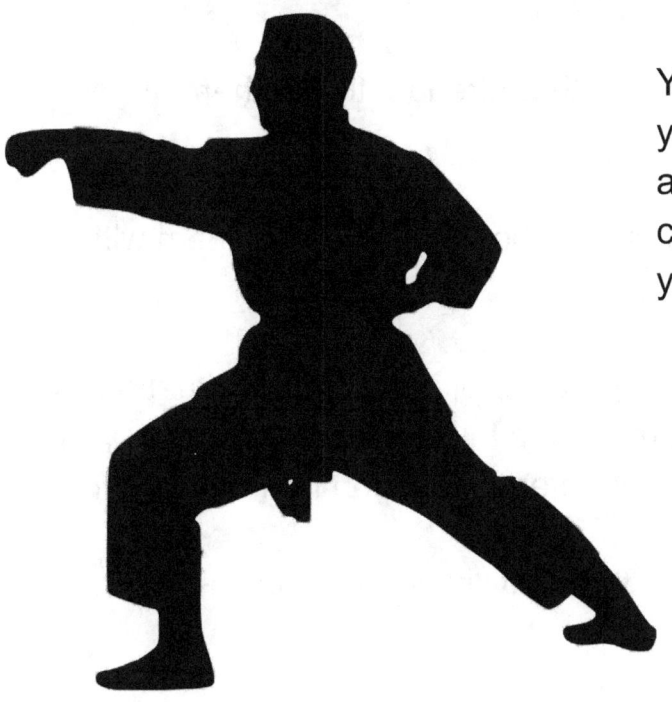

You want to create a machine in you. That detects an opportunity, and it unleashes the attack, counter, evasion program from your subconscious memory.

What I mean is this: Put down the combination of attacks you love (eg Kizami gyaku tsuki ura-mawashi geri), the counter patterns you love, the sweeping patterns you love, the throwing patterns you love, the feinting patterns you love etc.

Meditate over them frequently, practice them frequently, try them out on training partners.

Follow this pattern to the point where your body can express them without you thinking of what to do.

When your eyes see an attack coming at you or you sense a situation, you will not need to think of what to do (because thinking is slow), rather your body responds with the appropriate counter, or evasion for that scenario.

This is harmony (oneness) between the body, mind and spirit. Perfect communication.

But you only get here by meditating and practicing the patterns you love to use consistently.

Your body at this point has memorized your patterns and can freely express itself from your subconscious as you sense or your eyes see a situation that requires your response.

This is so powerful. And I like to say this: the most trained person is almost always the champion. Choose to be that person.

# CHAPTER 8

## Tactic 6: Never pass up opportunities to take advantage of your opponent's mistakes

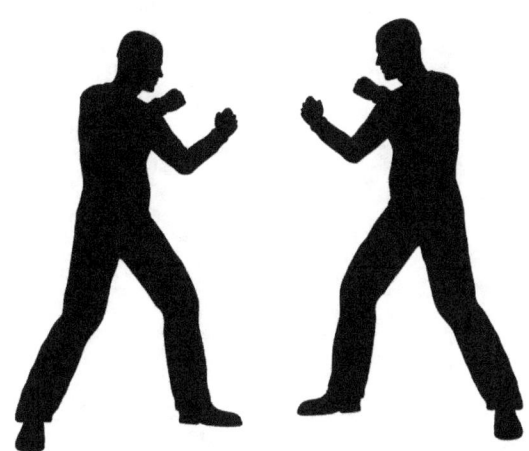

You want to be a kind of fighter that forces his or her opponents to make mistakes.

How do you do that?

By squeezing them, pulling them, feinting them, entering their circle of discomfort that will make them throw out something at you prematurely.

And that should always be your counter chance.

You have to train and prepare well for this so that you can always make clean and good scores.

Alternatively, even if you don't force your opponents to make errors, they will make a few of their own during a match.

You must be mentally ready to convert those chances.

Meditate on you taking advantage of the misses your opponents will make.
Hold that strong in your mind. Build it into your subconscious.
And be ready to just go for it when it occurs. Don't pass them by.
Those may be the only chances you would convert in a highly technical and difficult fight.

# Conclusion:

Just like every other field of endeavor, the top 1% are people who chose to master their craft and game.

If you follow these Tactics as foundation and consolidate on them, you will be among the top and few one percenters in your weight category globally.

This is proven over and over again. The tactics work.
However, the persons that will commit to it will gain the glory.

The top is not for everyone, and the journey is the distinguisher that separates the best from the rest.

I was among the best in my country and Africa. You too can be the best in the world if you make these tactics yours.

Own them, eat them! Remember, the best things are for the best athletes. The Gold medal and gigantic trophies, and even the cash prices and the fame and glory.

See you at the top!


**Appreciation:**

Thank you for getting this book. If you gained some value from it, kindly leave me a comment or two via my email: senseiefezino@gmail.com

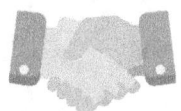

www.ingramcontent.com/pod-product-compliance
Lightning Source LLC
Chambersburg PA
CBHW080440220526
45465CB00009B/3359